Collins

AQA GCSE 9-1

English Language

Grade 5

English Language

AQA
GCSE 9-1

Exam Practice Workbook Grade 5

Jo Heathcote and Sheila McCann

Acknowledgements

The author and publisher are grateful to the copyright holders for permission to use quoted materials and images.

Article on pages 33–34 *The Queen's Diamond Jubilee: I have memories to treasure forever* by Gordon Rayner, The Telegraph, 5 June 2012 © Telegraph Media Group Limited 2012

All images © Shutterstock.com

Every effort has been made to trace copyright holders and obtain their permission for the use of copyright material. The author and publisher will gladly receive information enabling them to rectify any error or omission in subsequent editions. All facts are correct at time of going to press.

Published by Collins
An imprint of HarperCollins*Publishers*
1 London Bridge Street
London SE1 9GF

© HarperCollins*Publishers* Limited 2018

ISBN 9780008280963

First published 2018

10 9 8 7 6 5 4 3 2 1

British Library Cataloguing in Publication Data.

A CIP record of this book is available from the British Library.

Commissioning Editor: Kelly Ferguson
Authors: Jo Heathcote and Sheila McCann
Project Editor: Charlotte Christensen
Cover Design: Paul Oates
Inside Text Design and Layout: Ian Wrigley
Production: Natalia Rebow
Printed and bound by Martins The Printers

Contents

How to Use this Book

This workbook contains all of the source material and exam practice questions for both Paper 1 and Paper 2 of GCSE English Language. The sources and questions have been modelled on the ones you will sit in your AQA GCSE 9–1 English Language exam. Writing space has been included to allow you to write your answers in the book.

There are a couple of ways you can use this workbook.

1. **As a set of mock exams:**
   You could set aside the correct time slot for each paper and complete the examination-style questions under timed conditions. This will help you to experience what it will be like on the day of the real exam. It's a good idea to use the workbook in this way if you are already confident with your skills.

   Once you have completed each exam, there are sample answers and AQA-style mark scheme grids for you to match your own responses against. The relevant level has been shaded in green in the marking grids.

   A good way to check your response is to ask yourself if your own answer seems…
   - stronger than the sample response
   - weaker than the sample response
   - **or** similar to the sample response.

2. **As a step-by-step skills booster and revision programme:**
   Here you might focus on one question at a time. Remind yourself of the skills you think you need for each question. Read the 'Checklist for success' to help you with this. Write your own response.

   Once you have answered a question, carefully check your response against the sample answer, making notes for yourself in the 'My checklist for success' box of any skills you might have missed. Read the 'Commentary' box, which explains how the sample answer has been structured and what effect the writing has.

   In this way you can work at your own pace and spend more time on the questions you are unsure of in order to really boost your skills.

An ebook version of this workbook can be downloaded for free. For access to the ebook, visit **www.collins.co.uk/ebooks** and follow the step-by-step instructions.

Paper 1: Explorations in creative reading and writing

Paper 1 Overview

In *Paper 1 Explorations in creative reading and writing* there are two sections: **Section A Reading** and **Section B Writing**. Questions will be based on a Source, which will be one single text.

The maximum marks for this paper are 80 marks and the time allowed is 1 hour 45 minutes. You are advised to spend about 15 minutes reading through the Source and the five questions that you need to answer before you begin writing. You should also allow enough time at the end to read through / check your answers.

In Paper 1 Section A of the exam, you will be assessed on the quality of your **reading**. You will be asked to read a piece of source material from a short story or novel from the 20th or 21st century. You are unlikely to have seen the passage before.

Your job is to apply your skills of reading and analysis to answer the questions about the passage.

You are advised to spend about **1 hour** on this section. You need to read and complete **four** questions worth **40 marks** – half of the marks for the paper.

In Paper 1 Section B of the exam, you will be assessed on the quality of your **writing**. You will be asked to write an extended writing response to either a descriptive task or a narrative task.

You are advised to spend about **45 minutes** on this section. You need to complete **one** question worth **40 marks** – half of the marks for the paper. You will be awarded up to 24 marks for content and organisation, and up to 16 marks for technical accuracy.

Section A: Reading

Begin by reading carefully the extract below from *The Great Gatsby* by F. Scott Fitzgerald.

There was music from my neighbour's house through the summer nights. In his blue gardens men and girls came and went like moths among the whisperings and the champagne and the stars. At high tide in the afternoon I watched his guests diving from the tower of his raft, or taking the sun on the hot sand of his beach while his two motor-boats slit the waters of the Sound, drawing aquaplanes over

5 cataracts of foam. On week-ends his Rolls-Royce became an omnibus, bearing parties to and from the city between nine in the morning and long past midnight, while his station wagon scampered like a brisk yellow bug to meet all trains. And on Mondays eight servants, including an extra gardener, toiled all day with mops and scrubbing-brushes and hammers and garden-shears, repairing the ravages of the night before.

10 Every Friday five crates of oranges and lemons arrived from a fruiterer in New York — every Monday these same oranges and lemons left his back door in a pyramid of pulpless halves. There was a machine in the kitchen which could extract the juice of two hundred oranges in half an hour if a little button was pressed two hundred times by a butler's thumb.

At least once a fortnight a corps of caterers came down with several hundred feet of canvas and

15 enough colored lights to make a Christmas tree of Gatsby's enormous garden. On buffet tables, garnished with glistening hors-d'oeuvre, spiced baked hams crowded against salads of harlequin designs and pastry pigs and turkeys bewitched to a dark gold. In the main hall a bar with a real brass rail was set up, and stocked with gins and liquors and with cordials so long forgotten that most of his female guests were too young to know one from another.

20 By seven o'clock the orchestra has arrived, no thin five-piece affair, but a whole pitful of oboes and trombones and saxophones and viols and cornets and piccolos, and low and high drums. The last swimmers have come in from the beach now and are dressing up-stairs; the cars from New York are parked five deep in the drive, and already the halls and salons and verandas are gaudy with primary colors, and hair bobbed in strange new ways, and shawls beyond the dreams of Castile. The bar is

25 in full swing, and floating rounds of cocktails permeate the garden outside, until the air is alive with chatter and laughter, and casual innuendo and introductions forgotten on the spot, and enthusiastic meetings between women who never knew each other's names.

The lights grow brighter as the earth lurches away from the sun, and now the orchestra is playing yellow cocktail music, and the opera of voices pitches a key higher. Laughter is easier minute by

30 minute, spilled with prodigality, tipped out at a cheerful word. The groups change more swiftly, swell with new arrivals, dissolve and form in the same breath; already there are wanderers, confident girls who weave here and there among the stouter and more stable, become for a sharp, joyous moment the centre of a group, and then, excited with triumph, glide on through the sea-change of faces and voices and colour under the constantly changing light.

Now read the first examination task and write out your answer carefully.

This is testing your basic skills for AO1.

0 1 Read again the first part of the Source from **lines 1 to 10**.

List **four** things you learn from the extract about the narrator's neighbour. **[4 marks]**

Checklist for success

- Present your response to Question 1 in a numbered list.
- Use short, sharp, clear sentences.
- Use only things that are given to you in the extract and that you can identify as being true.

1. ....

....

....

2. ....

....

....

3. ....

....

....

4. ....

....

....

Section A: Reading

0 2 Look in detail at this section of the extract from **lines 14 to 27** of the Source.

How does the writer use language here to describe the neighbour's (Gatsby's) party?

At least once a fortnight a corps of caterers came down with several hundred feet of canvas and
15 enough colored lights to make a Christmas tree of Gatsby's enormous garden. On buffet tables,
garnished with glistening hors-d'oeuvre, spiced baked hams crowded against salads of harlequin
designs and pastry pigs and turkeys bewitched to a dark gold. In the main hall a bar with a real brass
rail was set up, and stocked with gins and liquors and with cordials so long forgotten that most of his
female guests were too young to know one from another.

20 By seven o'clock the orchestra has arrived, no thin five-piece affair, but a whole pitful of oboes and
trombones and saxophones and viols and cornets and piccolos, and low and high drums. The last
swimmers have come in from the beach now and are dressing up-stairs; the cars from New York are
parked five deep in the drive, and already the halls and salons and verandas are gaudy with primary
colors, and hair bobbed in strange new ways, and shawls beyond the dreams of Castile. The bar is
25 in full swing, and floating rounds of cocktails permeate the garden outside, until the air is alive with
chatter and laughter, and casual innuendo and introductions forgotten on the spot, and enthusiastic
meetings between women who never knew each other's names.

You could include the writer's choice of:
- words and phrases
- language features and techniques
- sentence forms.

[8 marks]

Checklist for success

- Select no more than three features of language.
- Make sure you give an example of each one.
- Make a comment that explains its effect by deciding on what it makes you think of, feel or imagine.

_____

_____

_____

_____

Section A: Reading

This is also testing your skills for AO2.

0 3 You now need to think about the **whole** of the Source.

This text is an extract from a novel.

How has the writer structured the text to interest you, as a reader?

You could write about:

- what the writer focuses your attention on at the beginning
- how and why the writer changes the focus as the Source develops
- any other structural features that interest you.

[8 marks]

Checklist for success

- Select no more than three features of structure.
- Give an example of each one or indicate where they are with a line reference.
- Make a comment that explains what the feature does to the text and the effect this has on you, the reader.

Section A: Reading

Carefully read the selected extract from *The Great Gatsby*.

At least once a fortnight a corps of caterers came down with several hundred feet of canvas and
15 enough colored lights to make a Christmas tree of Gatsby's enormous garden. On buffet tables, garnished with glistening hors-d'oeuvre, spiced baked hams crowded against salads of harlequin designs and pastry pigs and turkeys bewitched to a dark gold. In the main hall a bar with a real brass rail was set up, and stocked with gins and liquors and with cordials so long forgotten that most of his female guests were too young to know one from another.

20 By seven o'clock the orchestra has arrived, no thin five-piece affair, but a whole pitful of oboes and trombones and saxophones and viols and cornets and piccolos, and low and high drums. The last swimmers have come in from the beach now and are dressing up-stairs; the cars from New York are parked five deep in the drive, and already the halls and salons and verandas are gaudy with primary colors, and hair bobbed in strange new ways, and shawls beyond the dreams of Castile. The bar is
25 in full swing, and floating rounds of cocktails permeate the garden outside, until the air is alive with chatter and laughter, and casual innuendo and introductions forgotten on the spot, and enthusiastic meetings between women who never knew each other's names.

The lights grow brighter as the earth lurches away from the sun, and now the orchestra is playing yellow cocktail music, and the opera of voices pitches a key higher. Laughter is easier minute by
30 minute, spilled with prodigality, tipped out at a cheerful word. The groups change more swiftly, swell with new arrivals, dissolve and form in the same breath; already there are wanderers, confident girls who weave here and there among the stouter and more stable, become for a sharp, joyous moment the centre of a group, and then, excited with triumph, glide on through the sea-change of faces and voices and colour under the constantly changing light.

Now read your examination task for Question 4 and plan your answer carefully before writing it out. This is testing your skills for AO4.

0 4   Focus your answer on this second part of the Source.

A student, having read this section of the text, said: **"F. Scott Fitzgerald creates a real sense of wealth and glamour in his description."**

To what extent do you agree?

In your response you could:
- consider your own impression of Gatsby's party
- evaluate how the writer creates a sense of wealth and glamour
- support your opinions with quotations from the text.   **[20 marks]**

Checklist for success

- Use clear, supported statements to address 'your own impression'.
- Make inferences to show your understanding.
- Focus in on the writer's choices of language or structure to address 'how the writer creates…' and comment on the effect.

Section A: Reading

Section B: Writing

In this final section of your Paper 1 mock exam, you are going to complete Section B of the paper, testing AO5 and AO6 and representing 40 marks.

You are advised to spend 45 minutes on the exam task. You must write in full sentences.

You are reminded of the need to plan your answer.

You should leave enough time to check your work at the end.

Select and complete one of the tasks below.

0 5 You are going to enter a creative writing competition.

> **Either:** Write a description suggested by this picture.

Checklist for success

- Write a structured five-point plan.
- Remember to use topic sentences.
- Plan a selection of interesting language and structural features to include in the description.

Or: Write a short story about a time when a party or celebration went badly wrong.

(24 marks for content and organisation,
16 marks for technical accuracy)
[40 marks]

Checklist for success

- Ensure your story has an effective opening, a complication, a climax and resolution. Make sure these features are clearly paragraphed and linked.

Section B: Writing

Section B: Writing

Responses – Section A: Reading

0 1 Read again the first part of the Source from **lines 1 to 10**.

List **four** things you learn from the extract about the narrator's neighbour.   **[4 marks]**

Sample Response:

> 1. He had two motor-boats.
>
> 2. He owned a Rolls-Royce.
>
> 3. He also owned a yellow station wagon.
>
> 4. He had servants.

My checklist for success

When I answer this question I need to remember to:

- ....
- ....
- ....

Responses – Section A: Reading

0 2 Look in detail at this section of the extract from **lines 14 to 27** of the Source.

How does the writer use language here to describe the neighbour's (Gatsby's) party?

You could include the writer's choice of:
- words and phrases
- language features and techniques
- sentence forms.

[8 marks]

Marking Grid:

AO2	
Level 4 **Detailed, perceptive analysis** 7–8 marks	Shows detailed and perceptive understanding of language: • Analyses the effects of language • Selects a judicious range of textual detail • Makes sophisticated and accurate use of subject terminology
Level 3 **Clear, relevant explanation** 5–6 marks	Shows clear understanding of language: • Explains clearly the effects of language • Selects a range of relevant detail • Makes clear and accurate use of subject terminology
Level 2 **Some understanding and comment** 3–4 marks	Shows some understanding of language: • Attempts to comment on the effect of language • Selects some appropriate textual detail • Makes some use of subject terminology
Level 1 **Simple, limited comment** 1–2 marks	Shows simple awareness of language features: • Offers simple comment on effect of language • Selects simple references or examples • Makes simple use of subject terminology, not always appropriately

Sample Response:

Gatsby's party is made to sound like a big celebration through the use of the metaphor: 'enough coloured lights to make a Christmas tree of Gatsby's garden'. This makes me imagine a place filled with fairy lights and sparkle.

The writer uses a list of all of the foods: 'spiced baked hams', 'salads of harlequin designs'. These sound very special and make the reader imagine a delicious feast.

The writer uses a lot of descriptive phrases such as, 'five deep', 'full swing', 'enthusiastic meetings'. These phrases make the reader imagine how lively the party is and the writer emphasises this by using personification to describe the air as being, 'alive with chatter and laughter'. All of these things give the reader an impression of how amazing Gatby's party must have been.

Clear opening statement and language feature

Relevant quotation

Sensible comment on effect

Another language feature

Useful and relevant textual detail selected

Another sensible comment thinking about the reader

Specific and relevant examples given

Comment on effect with further language feature identified and exemplified clearly

Commentary

This answer uses some sensible choices of subject terminology, which are not complex in any way. These useful terms then all have clear, accurate examples to accompany them.

The comments on effect – the ones that show the impact on the reader – are clear and appropriate. They are sensible and do not slip into content or comprehension, but keep the focus on how the writer may affect us through his choices.

My checklist for success

When I answer this question I need to remember to:

- ....
- ....
- ....

Responses – Section A: Reading

0 3 You now need to think about the **whole** of the Source.

This text is an extract from a novel.

How has the writer structured the text to interest you, as a reader?

You could write about:

- what the writer focuses your attention on at the beginning
- how and why the writer changes the focus as the Source develops
- any other structural features that interest you.

[8 marks]

Marking Grid:

AO2	
Level 4 **Detailed, perceptive analysis** 7–8 marks	Shows detailed and perceptive understanding of structural features: • Analyses the effects of structure • Selects a judicious range of examples • Makes sophisticated and accurate use of subject terminology
Level 3 **Clear, relevant explanation** 5–6 marks	Shows clear understanding of structural features: • Explains clearly the effects of structural features • Selects a range of relevant examples • Makes clear and accurate use of subject terminology
Level 2 **Some understanding and comment** 3–4 marks	Shows some understanding of structural features • Attempts to comment on the effect of structural features • Selects some appropriate examples • Makes some use of subject terminology
Level 1 **Simple, limited comment** 1–2 marks	Shows simple awareness of structural features: • Offers simple comment on the effect of structural features • Selects simple references or examples • Makes simple use of subject terminology, not always appropriately

Sample Response:

The extract is structured as a first person narrative, 'my neighbour', 'I watched'. This perspective means the reader sees all of the preparations for the party and the party itself through the neighbour's eyes.

There are time references right the way through the extract, 'Every Friday', 'every Monday', 'On weekends', 'the summer nights'. It shows the reader that there is almost a set routine to the parties as the same things happen each time and are seen by the narrator. It also shows the reader that the party was not a one-off event but something that happened regularly each week.

In the first part of the extract the narrator uses past tense, 'his station wagon scampered', 'eight servants ...toiled' but then the tense changes to the present 'the air is alive with chatter'. This seems to make the reader feel like they are actually at the party and part of what is going on, almost experiencing it for themselves.

Subject term relevant to structure

Relevant supporting textual detail

A sensible comment on the effect of this perspective

Identifies a second aspect of structure

A range of textual detail to support

A sensible and clear explanation of the effect of time references

Some more clear and accurate subject terminology relevant to the structure of the extract

Again a range of relevant detail

Sensible and clear explanation of effect

Commentary

This answer selects three sensible structural features to work with: narrative perspective, time and tense. They all have examples, which are clear, sensible and accurate without being lengthy.

The comments on effect show that the student is thinking carefully about what those features are doing to the text before they write the comment on effect, which is then very clear and sensible as a result.

My checklist for success

When I answer this question I need to remember to:

-
-
-

Responses – Section A: Reading

0 4 Focus your answer on this second part of the Source.

A student, having read this section of the text, said: **"F. Scott Fitzgerald creates a real sense of wealth and glamour in his description."**

To what extent do you agree?

In your response, you could:
- consider your own impression of Gatsby's party
- evaluate how the writer creates a sense of wealth and glamour
- support your opinions with quotations from the text.

[20 marks]

Marking Grid:

AO4	
Level 4 **Perceptive, detailed evaluation** 16–20 marks	Shows perceptive and detailed evaluation: • Critically and in detail evaluates the effects • Shows perceptive understanding of writer's methods • Selects a judicious range of textual references • Develops a convincing and perceptive response to the focus of the task
Level 3 **Clear, relevant evaluation** 11–15 marks	Shows clear and relevant evaluation: • Clearly evaluates the effects • Shows clear understanding of writer's methods • Selects a range of relevant textual references • Makes a clear and relevant response to the focus of the task
Level 2 **Some evaluation** 6–10 marks	Shows some attempts at evaluation: • Makes some evaluative comment(s) on effect • Shows some understanding of writer's methods • Selects some appropriate textual references • Makes some response to the focus of the task
Level 1 **Simple, limited evaluation** 1–5 marks	Shows simple, limited evaluation: • Makes simple, limited evaluative comment(s) on effect(s) • Shows limited understanding of writer's methods • Selects simple, limited textual reference(s) • Makes a simple limited response to the focus of the statement

Sample Response:

I agree that the writer presents a very glamorous and wealthy scene in the extract. The food seems like a delicious banquet, 'buffet tables, glistening ..... dark gold.' This suggests that even the food sparkles like expensive jewels. The writer creates a semantic field of wealth by using adjectives such as 'glistening' and 'dark gold' to describe the food.

The guests at the party also seem to be very glamorous and fashionable, as they have their 'hair bobbed in strange new ways'. The writer uses noun phrases such as 'enthusiastic meetings' and 'confident girls' to describe the guests. This makes me imagine people who are always socialising and have money to spend on the latest fashions.

We know that Gatsby must be wealthy because of all of the extravagant things at his party. For example he hires 'a corps of caterers', 'a whole pitful of oboes and trombones and saxophones ...' and he has an 'enormous garden' to hold the party in. This suggests he has a huge house with a lot of land and space and can afford to pay for these massive parties. The writer uses a metaphor, 'enough coloured lights to make a Christmas tree of Gatsby's enormous garden' to emphasise how light, bright and glamorous the garden is and how wealthy Gatsby must be to own it.

Annotations (right margin):

- Makes a clear supported statement with support and an inference to make a good clear start.
- Identifies a method and uses subject terminology, adding in relevant examples.
- Makes a second clear point and uses a good choice of quotation to support the point.
- Another method with examples
- A clear and sensible comment on effect
- A good range of relevant textual detail supports this point.
- This is followed with another sensible inference to show what is understood.
- Identifies another of the writer's methods and clearly explains the effect as well as linking back to the key words in the task.

Commentary

All of the ideas in this response are clear and relevant. There are some very apt quotations used as evidence for the points, and the inferences show understanding and add weight to the agreement with the statement in the question. The answer is clear and organised in the way it links in the writer's methods, with correct examples. Their comments on effect are sensible.

My checklist for success

When I answer this question I need to remember to:

- ....
- ....
- ....

Responses – Section B: Writing

0 5   You are going to enter a creative writing competition.

Either:

Write a description suggested by this picture.

Or:

Write a short story about a time when a party or celebration went badly wrong.

(24 marks for content and organisation, 16 marks for technical accuracy)

[40 marks]

Marking Grid: 24 marks available for content and organisation

AO5	Content	Organisation
Upper Level 4 **Compelling,** **Convincing** 22–24 marks	• Register is convincing and compelling for audience • Assuredly matched to purpose • Extensive and ambitious vocabulary with sustained crafting of linguistic devices	• Varied and inventive use of structural features • Writing is compelling, incorporating a range of convincing and complex ideas • Fluently linked paragraphs with seamlessly integrated discourse markers
Lower Level 4 **Compelling,** **Convincing** 19–21 marks	• Register is convincing and matched to audience • Convincingly matched to purpose • Extensive vocabulary with evidence of conscious crafting of linguistic devices	• Varied and effective use of structural features • Writing is highly engaging, with a range of developed complex ideas • Consistently coherent paragraphs with integrated discourse markers
Upper Level 3 **Consistent,** **Clear** 16–18 marks	• Register is consistently matched to audience • Consistently matched to purpose • Increasingly sophisticated vocabulary chosen for effect, range of successful linguistic devices	• Effective structural features • Engaging with a range of clear, connected ideas • Coherent paragraphs; integrated discourse markers
Lower Level 3 **Consistent,** **Clear** 13–15 marks	• Register is generally matched to audience • Generally matched to purpose • Vocabulary clearly chosen for effect; appropriate linguistic devices	• Usually effective structural features • Engaging with a range of connected ideas • Usually coherent paragraphs; a range of discourse markers
Upper Level 2 **Some success** 10–12 marks	• Sustained attempt to match register to audience • Sustained attempt to match purpose • Conscious use of vocabulary; some linguistic devices	• Some structural features • Variety of linked, relevant ideas • Some use of paragraphs and discourse markers

AO4	Content	Organisation
Lower Level 2 **Some success** 7–9 marks	• Attempts to match register to audience • Attempts to match purpose • Begins to vary vocabulary; some linguistic devices	• Attempts structural features • Some linked, relevant ideas • Attempts paragraphs with some markers
Upper Level 1 **Simple,** **Limited** 4–6 marks	• Simple awareness of register/audience • Simple awareness of purpose • Simple vocabulary and linguistic devices	• Evidence of simple structural features • One or two relevant ideas; simply linked • Random paragraph structure
Lower Level 1 **Limited** 1–3 marks	• Occasional sense of audience • Occasional sense of purpose • Simple vocabulary	• Limited or no evidence of structural features • One or two unlinked ideas • No paragraphs

Marking Grid: 16 marks available for technical accuracy

AO6	Skills Descriptors
Level 4 13–16 marks	• Sentence demarcation is consistently accurate • Wide range of punctuation used with accuracy • Uses wide range of sentence forms for effect • Uses Standard English consistently with secure control of structures • Accurate ambitious spellings • Ambitious and extensive vocabulary
Level 3 9–12 marks	• Sentence demarcation is mostly secure and mostly accurate • Range of punctuation is used, mostly with success • Uses a variety of sentence forms for effect • Mostly uses Standard English appropriately with mostly controlled grammatical structures • Generally accurate spelling, including complex and irregular words • Increasingly sophisticated use of vocabulary
Level 2 5–8 marks	• Sentence demarcation is mostly secure and sometimes accurate • Some control of a range of punctuation • Attempts a variety of sentence forms • Some use of Standard English with some control of agreement • Some accurate spelling of more complex words • Varied use of vocabulary
Level 1 1–4 marks	• Occasional use of sentence demarcation • Some evidence of conscious punctuation • Simple range of sentence forms • Occasional use of Standard English with limited control of agreement • Accurate basic spelling • Simple use of vocabulary

Responses – Section B: Writing

Sample Response 1: Descriptive task

It was a perfect day.

The sun shone down on the beautiful, magical castle like a Disney fairytale come to life. The castle had red rooftops made up of tiny tiles and turrets looking neat and perfect against the sky.

The castle had cream painted walls like vanilla ice cream, just perfect in the bright, crisp sunshine. The castle towers upwards like a wedding cake just waiting to be sliced and it brings joy and happiness to everyone who looks on it.

The castle has a million tiny windows looking out onto the sparkling, glinting water – as calm as calm can be. Who could be behind them I wonder? I imagine grand duchesses from the past in velvet gowns, or bored princesses waiting to be rescued.

The water in the lake looks so inviting; you could just jump into it and swim from the jumping off point out of the front of the castle.

Right the way around the castle there are lush, tropical trees making it look cool and shady. It looks like there are little secret paths in the bushes and trees. You can imagine in the past the lords and ladies taking a stroll through there or children running and hiding.

Behind the castle are big, tall mountains all covered in bushes and trees. They are like guards, keeping the castle hidden from the outside world. The castle is a hideaway, a secret place in the forest now; perhaps for film stars or celebrities to escape the paparazzi and have some peace.

The writing is already showing it is descriptive and the sentences are clearly punctuated.

There are a number of linguistic devices used here (i.e. similes) and the work is using paragraphs clearly.

You can now see a sequence or structure to the description and it is still matching purpose by describing and not telling a story.

There is a good variety of vocabulary and a more complex punctuation mark is used accurately.

There is an added idea here, which is linked and relevant and more interesting vocabulary is used.

Another interesting simile used. The writing is clear all the way through and in Standard English.

There are some accurate, complex spellings in the writing and a sense of a structure with the ending.

Commentary

This piece is organised very clearly into paragraphs and has a good sense of a structure. It describes all the way through, like an outside observer, and does not slip into telling a story at all. There are a number of good descriptive adjectives used and some linguistic features (similes) added for effect. There is a good range of vocabulary used right the way through. All of the sentences are clear and punctuated and there are some complex spellings too.

My checklist for success

When I answer this question I need to remember to:

- ....
- ....
- ....

Sample Response 2: Narrative task

It was the big day. Alice, the little princess, was turning 6. "Perfect Parties" had been booked to organise everything as both Anna and her husband had been working full time recently. They'd picked everything from the glamorous website, the cake, the themed food and the entertainers and it had all been paid for in advance. Nothing was too much for the little princess. The morning had been mostly spent playing with all Alice's new toys but now as the afternoon drew on they needed to get Alice into her special new party dress and get ready to leave.

They arrived at the church hall early, wanting to make sure they were the first ones there and ensure everything was perfect. Alice was bouncing up and down like a jack rabbit. They walked inside and looked around. The room was empty. Deserted. Surprised, Anna looked at her phone but there was no message from the company she'd hired to run the party and they'd specifically said that they would text her if anything went wrong. A few minutes went by and the first children started arriving. A little nervous now she sent an email to the company asking if everything was OK. Acting like it was nothing she moved back over to the new arrivals and said she assumed they were just running a bit late.

The final stragglers arrived and now twenty children were catapulting themselves around the room, getting very restless. The parents staying with their kids stood off to one side talking amongst themselves and looking rather disappointed.

Anxiety start to creep in as she stood there checking her phone as minutes flew by. There was still no response from the company. She called the number she'd been given in case of emergencies. The line rang dead and she heard an automated voice telling her that the number she was calling did not exist.

Slowly realising what had happened, she began to tell the other parents what had happened and attempted to come up with a solution. None presented itself and eventually the police were called. Disappointed children began filing out of the hall but most disappointed of all was the birthday girl. She sat in the back of the car, an air of misery about her. The presents sat unopened in the boot, almost forgotten about. They took her out for birthday pizza instead but it was unlikely the event of the day would ever be forgotten.

Annotations:
- Sets up a believable plot and creates a sense of the characters.
- Organises the work into paragraphs and creates a sense of structure and time passing.
- Adds some linguistic features to add a sense of the atmosphere.
- Uses a variety of sentences to create the appropriate tone.
- Uses some interesting vocabulary.
- Uses some engaging details to keep the reader's interest.
- Sustains the plot and brings the story to a neat conclusion.

Commentary

This is a clear and well-organised narrative, which is well planned and thought through. In clear paragraphs, the story creates a believable plot, which is well controlled and sensible in the time. As a result it has an effective conclusion. There is some use of interesting vocabulary to create a sense of the characters and their feelings and sentence variety is used effectively. Work is accurate and shows complex spelling and is constructed in Standard English throughout.

My checklist for success

When I answer this question I need to remember to:

- ....

Paper 2: Writers' viewpoints and perspectives

Paper 2 Overview

In *Paper 2 Writers' viewpoints and perspectives* there are two sections: **Section A Reading** and **Section B Writing**. Questions will be based on Sources, which will be two linked texts.

The maximum marks for this paper are 80 marks and the time allowed is 1 hour 45 minutes. You are advised to spend about 15 minutes reading through the two Sources and the five questions that you need to answer before you begin writing. You should also allow enough time at the end to read through / check your answers.

In Paper 2 Section A of the exam, you will be assessed on the quality of your **reading**. You will be asked to read two pieces of source material from non-fiction texts. One will be from the 19th century and the other will be more modern, from either the 20th or 21st century. You are unlikely to have seen the passages before.

Your job is to apply your skills of reading and analysis to answer the questions about the sources.

You are advised to spend about **1 hour** on this section. You need to read and complete four questions worth **40 marks** – half of the marks for the paper.

In Paper 2 Section B of the exam, you will be assessed on the quality of your **writing**. You will be asked to write an extended writing response presenting a viewpoint.

You are advised to spend about **45 minutes** on this section. You need to complete **one** question worth **40 marks** – half of the marks for the paper. You will be awarded up to 24 marks for content and organisation, and up to 16 marks for technical accuracy.

Section A: Reading

Begin by reading the extract below carefully. It is a broadsheet newspaper article about Queen Elizabeth II's Diamond Jubilee in 2015 celebrating the Queen's 60-year reign.

Source A

The Queen's Diamond Jubilee: I have memories to treasure forever

The Queen has described the public's ecstatic response to her **Diamond Jubilee** as "a humbling experience" as she thanked the nation at the climax of a spectacular weekend of celebration.

In a rare televised address to Britain and the Commonwealth, the sovereign said she would "treasure" the memories of the past week.

5 For the third consecutive day, hundreds of thousands of people flooded into the capital to pay tribute to "Elizabeth the Great" as one banner described her.

The Queen was visibly moved as she stepped out onto the balcony of Buckingham Palace to see The Mall filled with people who had, once again, shrugged off cold and rain to cheer her on.

"Oh my goodness, how extraordinary!" Her Majesty said as she saw the ocean of red, white and blue
10 stretching as far as the eye could see.

Only six members of the Royal family appeared on the balcony, and as a statement of the endurance of the monarchy, it could not have been bolder.

Flanked by her heir, the Prince of Wales, and his eventual successor, the Duke of Cambridge, the Queen used the deliberately pared-down balcony appearance to tell the nation its future is in safe
15 hands. By showing the world the future of the monarchy, starting with the Prince of Wales, she was also delivering a clear message that there is no question of the succession skipping a generation.

She described the throng serenading her in The Mall with the National Anthem as "marvellous" and "incredible". Her only regret was that the Duke of Edinburgh, recovering in hospital from a bladder infection, was not by her side. "She's missing him, obviously," the Earl of Wessex said after a brief
20 hospital visit

In her televised address, one of only a handful she has made outside her traditional Christmas message, she said:

"The events that I have attended to mark my Diamond Jubilee have been a humbling experience."

"It has touched me deeply to see so many thousands of families, neighbours and friends celebrating
25 together in such a happy atmosphere."

She said she and the Duke of Edinburgh wanted to pass on their "special thanks" to the organisers of the events, which had been a "massive challenge".

She said: "I hope that memories of all this year's happy events will brighten our lives for many years to

come. I will continue to treasure and draw inspiration from the countless kindnesses shown to me in
30 this country and throughout the Commonwealth. Thank you all."

On a day when the fun of the previous three days gave way to more formal celebrations, the Queen decided that those in the direct line of succession should take centre stage.

The Prince of Wales and Duchess of Cornwall, the Duke and Duchess of Cambridge and Prince Harry were the only members of the Royal family who walked with her down the aisle for a Service
35 of Thanksgiving, lunched with her at Westminster Hall and drove through London in open carriages before their 11-minute balcony appearance.

Aides said the Queen wanted the nation, and the watching world, to concentrate on the future of the monarchy, and it was a message that was received loud and clear.

The day began with the service at St Paul's Cathedral, attended by a congregation of 2,000 invited
40 guests including more than 50 members of the Royal family.

Then came the moment those lining the streets had been waiting for since the early morning, or even overnight – the carriage procession, accompanied by more than 100 guardsmen on horseback in full dress uniform.

After driving down Whitehall and rounding the corner of Trafalgar Square, the procession entered The
45 Mall, lined by hundreds of guardsmen in bearskins and red tunics, and crowds standing 10 to 20 deep.

Then, at 3.25pm, the doors behind the balcony opened and the Queen made her appearance, beaming and waving at the masses below.

"It's a marvellous time," the Queen said as she waved again to the crowd after the National Anthem. The Duke of Cambridge leaned to her and said "[listen to] to those cheers for you". Finally, as she
50 turned to go back inside, she added: "Incredible people. Bless them."

Gordon Rayner, The Telegraph, 5 June 2012

Now read your first examination task and respond carefully.

This is testing your basic skills for AO1.

0 1 Read again the first part of **Source A** from **lines 1 to 12**.

Choose **four** statements below that are TRUE.

- Shade the boxes of the ones that you think are true
- Choose a maximum of four statements   **[4 marks]**

A   The Queen thanked the nation at the beginning of the weekend.

B   Hundreds of people gathered to see the Queen.

C   The Queen was celebrating her Diamond Jubilee.

D   The Queen did not move as she stood on the balcony.

E   It is rare for the Queen to speak to the nation on television.

F   The Queen greeted well-wishers from the balcony of Buckingham Palace.

G   The Queen was looking out towards the ocean.

H   She appeared with six members of her family.

Checklist for success

- Skim and scan to locate the relevant information in the extract.
- Be aware that the wording of the statement may be different from the information in the extract.
- Use your skills of inference to decide if the statement is true or false.

Section A: Reading

Source B

A never to be forgotten day. No one ever I believe, has met with such an ovation as was given to me, passing through those 6 miles of streets, including Constitution Hill. The crowds were quite indescribable & their enthusiasm truly marvellous & deeply touching. The cheering was quite deafening, & every face seemed to be filled with real joy. I was much moved & gratified…I started from the State

5 Entrance in an open state landau, drawn by 8 creams, dear Alix, looking very pretty in lilac, & Lenchen, sitting opposite me. I felt a good deal agitated, & had been so all these days, for fear anything might be forgotten or go wrong. Bertie & George C. rode one on each side of the carriage, Arthur (who had charge of the whole military arrangements) a little in the rear…Before leaving I touched an electric button, by which I started a message which was telegraphed throughout the whole Empire.

10 It was the following: "From my heart I thank my beloved people, may God bless them". At this time the sun burst out. Vicky was in the carriage nearest to me, not being able to go in mine, as her rank as Empress prevented her sitting with her back to the horses, for I had to sit alone. Her carriage was drawn up by 4 blacks, richly caparisoned in red. We went up Constitution Hill & Piccadilly & there were seats right along the former, where my own servants & personal attendants, & members of the

15 other Royal Households, the Chelsea Pensioners & the children of the Duke of York's & Greenwich schools had seats. St James' Street was beautifully decorated with festoons of flowers across the road, & many loyal inscriptions. Trafalgar Square was very striking & outside the National Gallery stands were erected for the House of Lords. The denseness of the crowds was immense, but the order maintained wonderful. The streets in the Strand are now quite wide, but one misses Temple Bar.

20 Here, the Lord Mayor received me & presented the sword, which I touched. He then immediately mounted his horse, in his robes & galloped [sic] past bare headed carrying the sword, preceding my carriage accompanied by his Sheriffs. As we neared St Paul's the Procession was often stopped, & the crowds broke out into singing "God Save The Queen". In one house were assembled the survivors of the Charge of Balaclava. In front of the Cathedral, the scene was most impressive. All the Colonial

25 troops, on foot, were drawn up round the Square. My carriage, surrounded by all the Royal Princes was drawn up close to the steps, where the Clergy were assembled, the Bishops, in rich copes, with their croziers, the Arch Bishop of Canterbury & the Bishop of London, each holding a very fine one. A Te Deum was sung, especially composed by Dr Martin, the Lord's Prayer, most beautifully chanted, a special Jubilee prayer, & the benediction concluded the short service, preceded by the singing of the

30 old 100th, in which everyone joined. "God Save The Queen" was also sung…

Royal Archives, British Monarchy website

0 2 You need to refer to **Source A** and **Source B** for this question:

The ways in which Queen Victoria and Queen Elizabeth II celebrated their Diamond Jubilees were similar.

Use details from **both** sources to write a summary of the similarities. **[8 marks]**

Checklist for success

- Make clear statements in your own words, addressing the question directly.
- Support those statements with selected quotations.
- Make inferences to show your understanding.
- Remember this is an 8-mark short-answer task.

Section A: Reading

0 3 You now need to refer only to **Source B**, Queen Victoria's journal entry about her Jubilee celebration. (Use **lines 1 to 11** below.)

How does Queen Victoria use language to convey her feelings about the Diamond Jubilee celebrations? **[12 marks]**

A never to be forgotten day. No one ever I believe, has met with such an ovation as was given to me, passing through those 6 miles of streets, including Constitution Hill. The crowds were quite indescribable & their enthusiasm truly marvellous & deeply touching. The cheering was quite deafening, & every face seemed to be filled with real joy. I was much moved & gratified…I started from the State

5 Entrance in an open state landau, drawn by 8 creams, dear Alix, looking very pretty in lilac, & Lenchen, sitting opposite me. I felt a good deal agitated, & had been so all these days, for fear anything might be forgotten or go wrong. Bertie & George C. rode one on each side of the carriage, Arthur (who had charge of the whole military arrangements) a little in the rear…Before leaving I touched an electric button, by which I started a message which was telegraphed throughout the whole Empire.

10 It was the following: "From my heart I thank my beloved people, may God bless them". At this time the sun burst out.

Checklist for success
- In this response, select no more than four language features.
- Make sure you give an example of each one.
- Make a comment that explains what the feature is actually doing.
- Develop that comment by deciding on what it makes you think of, feel or imagine.

Section A: Reading

Section A: Reading

This question is testing your skills for AO3.

It represents 16 of the 40 marks for Section A.

You will find it helpful to re-read both of the extracts before you begin.

Question 4 will ask you to focus on both pieces of source material and select your ideas from anywhere in the Sources.

Carefully read your examination task for Question 4 and plan your answer using the bullet points to guide you.

0 4 For this question, you need to refer to the **whole of Source A** together with the **whole of Source B**.

Compare how the writers have conveyed their different ideas and perspectives about the Diamond Jubilee celebrations.

In your response you could:
- compare their perspectives on the Diamond Jubilees
- compare the methods they use to present the ideas and perspectives
- support your ideas with quotations from both texts.   **[16 marks]**

Checklist for success
- Understand and explain the key connections between the two texts.
- Use the AO1 S.Q.I. structure (Statement, Quotation, Inference).
- Lead into an AO2 point (writer's method + example + effect).
- Use **both/however/whereas** to structure your comparison.

Section A: Reading

Section B: Writing

In this final section of your Paper 2 mock exam, you are going to complete Section B of the paper, testing AO5 and AO6 and worth 40 marks. There will be one task to respond to.

Remember:
- *you are advised to spend 45 minutes on the exam task*
- *you must write in full sentences*
- *you are reminded of the need to plan your answer*
- *you should leave enough time to check your work at the end.*

0 5   Some people think the Royal Family are an important part of British heritage and tradition; others feel they are a costly waste of taxpayers' money.

Write a speech for a debate in your school or college about whether the Royal Family should be a part of Britain's future or whether it should be abolished.

(24 marks for content and organisation,

16 marks for technical accuracy)

[40 marks]

Checklist for success

A successful response should include:
- a clear sense of your point of view and your reasons for it
- a convincing argument, supported by well-developed ideas
- language style and rhetorical features matched to the task and audience
- a structure that is persuasive and logical.

Section B: Writing

Section B: Writing

0 1 Read again the first part of **Source A** from **lines 1 to 12**.

Choose **four** statements below that are TRUE.

- Shade the boxes of the ones that you think are true
- Choose a maximum of four statements   **[4 marks]**

A The Queen thanked the nation at the beginning of the weekend.	◯
B Hundreds of people gathered to see the Queen.	◯
C The Queen was celebrating her Diamond Jubilee.	◯
D The Queen did not move as she stood on the balcony.	◯
E It is rare for the Queen to speak to the nation on television.	◯
F The Queen greeted well-wishers from the balcony of Buckingham Palace.	◯
G The Queen was looking out towards the ocean.	◯
H She appeared with six members of her family.	◯

Sample Response:

C The Queen was celebrating her Diamond Jubilee.	⬤
E It is rare for the Queen to speak to the nation on television.	⬤
F The Queen greeted well-wishers from the balcony of Buckingham Palace.	⬤
H She appeared with six members of her family.	⬤

Commentary

The following statements are incorrect because:

A It mentions the 'climax' of the weekend, meaning at the end of it.

B It was actually hundreds of thousands of people.

D It says she was 'visibly moved', suggesting she was emotionally affected and that this could be seen by her actions.

G The word 'ocean' is being used metaphorically, suggesting all she can see is a vast number of Union Jack flags before her.

My checklist for success

When I answer this question I need to remember to:

- ....
- ....
- ....

Responses – Section A: Reading

0 2 You need to refer to **Source A** and **Source B** for this question:

The ways in which Queen Victoria and Queen Elizabeth II celebrated their Diamond Jubilees were similar.

Use details from **both** sources to write a summary of the similarities.   **[8 marks]**

Marking Grid:

AO1	
Level 4 **Perceptive summary** 7–8 marks	Shows clear synthesis and interpretation of both texts: • Makes perceptive inferences from both texts • Makes judicious references/use of textual detail to the focus of the question • Statements show perceptive similarities between texts
Level 3 **Clear, relevant summary** 5–6 marks	Shows clear synthesis and interpretation of both texts: • Makes clear inferences from both texts • Selects clear quotations/textual details relevant to the focus of the task • Statements show clear similarities between texts
Level 2 **Some attempts at summary** 3–4 marks	Shows some interpretation from one/both texts: • Attempts some inference(s) from one/both texts • Selects some appropriate quotations/textual detail from one/both texts • Statements show some similarities between texts
Level 1 **Simple, limited summary** 1–2 marks	Shows simple awareness from one/both texts: • Offers paraphrase rather than inference • Makes simple reference/textual details from one/both texts • Statements show simple similarities between texts

Sample Response:

For both celebrations, lots of people turned up to celebrate the Queens' Diamond Jubilees. In Source A it says 'hundreds of thousands of people flooded into the capital.' This suggests the event was very popular and many people wanted to come and show their love or respect for the Queen on that day.

Similarly, Queen Victoria wrote in her diary, 'The denseness of the crowd was immense' and that no-one 'has met with such an ovation as was given to me.' This suggests she feels really surprised at the way people have come to show their respect and appreciation.

Both celebrations involved going to St Paul's Cathedral with lots of people attending. 'A congregation of 2000 invited guests' were at Queen Elizabeth's celebration' and Queen Victoria talks about bishops as well as Royal Princes being there, which shows both of these were large and important parts of the day.

In Queen Elizabeth's case it talks about a thanksgiving service suggesting the Queen perhaps feels grateful that she has been a monarch for 60 years whereas in Victoria's diary the emphasis seems to be more on the ceremony of the occasion, 'rich copes' 'a special jubilee prayer', suggesting that it is her role that is being celebrated.

A clear statement of a similarity, supported by relevant quotations and followed with a straightforward but clear inference.

A second inference from Source B.

Another clear statement of similarity, supported in two different ways from both texts.

A second inference from Source A.

Commentary

This response makes two very clear statements of similarity. These are both supported with either quotations or relevant specific details from the text.

There are clear inferences or suggestions made from both texts to show understanding of what is similar about both celebrations.

My checklist for success

When I answer this question I need to remember to:

- ....
- ....
- ....
- ....

0 3 You now need to refer only to **Source B**, Queen Victoria's journal entry about her Jubilee celebration. (Use **lines 1 to 11.**)

How does Queen Victoria use language to convey her feelings about the Diamond Jubilee celebrations?   **[12 marks]**

Marking Grid:

AO2	
Level 4 **Detailed, perceptive analysis** 10–12 marks	Shows detailed and perceptive understanding of language: • Analyses the effects of language • Selects a judicious range of textual detail • Makes sophisticated and accurate use of subject terminology
Level 3 **Clear, relevant explanation** 7–9 marks	Shows clear understanding of language: • Explains clearly the effects of language • Selects a range of relevant detail • Makes clear and accurate use of subject terminology
Level 2 **Some understanding and comment** 4–6 marks	Shows some understanding of language: • Attempts to comment on the effect of language • Selects some appropriate textual detail • Makes some use of subject terminology, mainly appropriately
Level 1 **Simple, limited comment** 1–3 marks	Shows simple awareness of language: • Offers simple comments on the effects of language • Selects simple references or textual details • Makes simple use of subject terminology, not always appropriately

Sample Response:

The writer uses a range of interesting adjectives to describe the crowds and their response to her such as 'marvellous' and 'touching.' All of these have the effect of showing Victoria's wonder at the crowd's response and also that she is a little bit overwhelmed by it.

She also uses adjectives to describe the range of feelings she had when seeing the crowds: 'moved, gratified, agitated'. This makes me imagine that she would have had a mix of feelings and that she was probably quite nervous about everything. This helps the reader understand that even for a queen it would have been quite a stressful event.

Victoria uses lots of proper nouns in her diary, which are of people: 'George C', 'Bertie', 'Alix', 'Lenchen'. This gives the impression that this is a very personal piece of writing where she does not need to spell out the detail as she will recognise these names as they are people who are close to her.

There are a number of more unusual formal words used such as the noun 'ovation'. 'Ovation' sounds a lot more formal than 'cheering' but it creates the effect that the crowds were really pleased to see the Queen and she is really touched by it.

A language feature has been identified and examples given.

A clear explanation of the possible effect of the language chosen.

More accurate subject terminology with correct examples.

Another sensible explanation of possible effect of the choice made.

Commentary

Throughout the answer there is a range of sensible subject terminology, which is used accurately and supported with relevant examples. Their comments on the effect of language on the reader have been clearly explained and are clear and sensible.

My checklist for success

When I answer this question I need to remember to:

-
-
-
-

0 4 For this question, you need to refer to the **whole of Source A** together with the **whole of Source B**.

Compare how the writers have conveyed their different ideas and perspectives about the Diamond Jubilee celebrations.

In your response you could:
- compare their perspectives on the Diamond Jubilees
- compare the methods they use to present the ideas and perspectives
- support your ideas with quotations from both texts.

[16 marks]

Marking Grid:

AO3	
Level 4 **Perceptive, detailed comparison** 13–16 marks	• Compares ideas and perspectives in a perceptive way • Analyses how writers' methods are used • Selects a range of judicious textual detail from both texts • Shows a detailed understanding of the different ideas and perspectives in both texts
Level 3 **Clear, relevant comparison** 9–12 marks	• Compares ideas and perspectives in a clear and relevant way • Explains clearly how writers' methods are used • Selects relevant detail to support comparisons from both texts • Shows a clear understanding of the different ideas and perspectives in both texts
Level 2 **Some comparison** 5–8 marks	• Attempts to compare ideas and perspectives • Makes some comment on how writers' methods are used • Selects some appropriate textual detail from one or both texts • Identifies some different ideas and perspectives
Level 1 **Simple, limited comparison** 1–4 marks	• Makes simple cross reference of ideas and perspectives • Makes simple identification of writers' methods • Makes simple references/textual details from one or both texts • Shows simple awareness of ideas and/or perspectives

Sample Response:

The two texts are written from very different perspectives. Source B describes both what happened and the feelings Queen Victoria had on the day of her diamond jubilee in her own words, 'I was much moved and gratified...'which suggests that she was overwhelmed by the experience of the day.

Victoria uses the adjective 'indescribable' to show the size of the crowd and also describes the cheering as 'deafening'. Both adjectives make me imagine how overwhelmed she is by the response she has received.

In contrast the reader of Source A is informed about the crowd and their response to the Queen through the eyes of an onlooker, 'For the third consecutive day, hundreds of thousands of people flooded into the capital' suggesting how popular and well-loved the Queen is. The writer of the article uses the adjective 'ecstatic' and also the metaphor 'the ocean of red, white and blue' suggesting that all that can be seen is a vast expanse of Union Jack flags being waved by a massive crowd of very enthusiastic supporters.

In Source A, the Queen is shown as sharing the day with her family, 'Flanked by her heir, the Prince of Wales' showing that her children were with her but not her husband who was in hospital, 'recovering .... from a bladder infection'. This implies it was a joyful occasion for the whole family, but maybe the Queen was missing her husband at the event. The writer uses the formal titles such as 'Duke of Edinburgh' and 'Earl of Wessex' to make the piece feel formal and respectful. However, because she is writing for herself Queen Victoria uses first names 'Alix,' 'Bertie,' and 'Vicky' which shows she knows who she is referring to as these may be her children. Queen Victoria also seems to be sharing the day with her family as she tells us that they were 'sitting opposite me' in the carriage.

In Source A, the Queen is overjoyed when the crowds start singing and 'serenading her ...with the National Anthem' which suggests the crowd is very patriotic and loves the Queen. In Source B, the crowds also 'broke out into singing "God save the Queen" which suggests that both Queens were loved and respected.

Annotations (right margin)

A clear opening statement, which is supported, and a useful inference is made.

This is linked with a language point exploring one of the methods Queen Victoria uses in her writing.

A linking supported statement brings in the second source and again makes a useful inference.

There is a further comment on method, this time from Source A.

There is a useful comparative point about naming in both texts, which adds to the work on methods in both sources.

The piece concludes with a final comparison of a linking idea, supported and with an overall inference.

Commentary

There is a clear understanding of the different viewpoints in each text shown by the number of clear supported statements. All of the statements are supported with relevant quotations. There are a number of inferences and suggestions made to show the texts are understood. These lead to a number of points about the writers' methods with references to adjectives, metaphors and formal titles. There are also the beginnings of some clear explanations of the possible effects of these on the reader.

My checklist for success

When I answer this question I need to remember to:

- ....
- ....
- ....
- ....

0 5 Some people think the Royal Family are an important part of British heritage and tradition; others feel they are a costly waste of taxpayers' money.

Write a speech for a debate in your school or college about whether the Royal Family should be a part of Britain's future or whether it should be abolished.

(24 marks for content and organisation,

16 marks for technical accuracy)

[40 marks]

Marking Grid: 24 marks available for content and organisation

AO5	Content	Organisation
Upper Level 4 **Compelling, Convincing** 22–24 marks	• Register is convincing and compelling for audience • Assuredly matched to purpose • Extensive and ambitious vocabulary with sustained crafting of linguistic devices	• Varied and inventive use of structural features • Writing is compelling, incorporating a range of convincing and complex ideas • Fluently linked paragraphs with seamlessly integrated discourse markers
Lower Level 4 **Compelling, Convincing** 19–21 marks	• Register is convincing and matched to audience • Convincingly matched to purpose • Extensive vocabulary with evidence of conscious crafting of linguistic devices	• Varied and effective use of structural features • Writing is highly engaging, with a range of developed complex ideas • Consistently coherent paragraphs with integrated discourse markers
Upper Level 3 **Consistent, Clear** 16–18 marks	• Register is consistently matched to audience • Consistently matched to purpose • Increasingly sophisticated vocabulary chosen for effect, range of successful linguistic devices	• Effective structural features • Engaging with a range of clear, connected ideas • Coherent paragraphs; integrated discourse markers
Lower Level 3 **Consistent, Clear** 13–15 marks	• Register is generally matched to audience • Generally matched to purpose • Vocabulary clearly chosen for effect; appropriate linguistic devices	• Usually effective structural features • Engaging with a range of connected ideas • Usually coherent paragraphs; a range of discourse markers
Upper Level 2 **Some success** 10–12 marks	• Sustained attempt to match register to audience • Sustained attempt to match purpose • Conscious use of vocabulary; some linguistic devices	• Some structural features • Variety of linked, relevant ideas • Some paragraphs and discourse markers
Lower Level 2 **Some success** 7–9 marks	• Attempts to match register to audience • Attempts to match purpose • Begins to vary vocabulary; some linguistic devices	• Attempts structural features • Some linked, relevant ideas • Attempts paragraphs with some markers

AO4	Content	Organisation
Upper Level 1 Simple, Limited 4–6 marks	• Simple awareness of register/audience • Simple awareness of purpose • Simple vocabulary and linguistic devices	• Evidence of simple structural features • One or two relevant ideas; simply linked • Random paragraph structure
Lower Level 1 Simple, Limited 1–3 marks	• Occasional sense of audience • Occasional sense of purpose • Simple vocabulary	• Limited or no evidence of structural features • One or two unlinked ideas • No paragraphs

Marking Grid: 16 marks available for technical accuracy

AO6	Skills Descriptors
Level 4 13–16 marks	• Sentence demarcation is consistently accurate • Wide range of punctuation used with accuracy • Uses wide range of sentence forms for effect • Uses Standard English consistently with secure control of structures • Accurate ambitious spellings • Ambitious and extensive vocabulary
Level 3 9–12 marks	• Sentence demarcation is mostly secure and mostly accurate • Range of punctuation is used, mostly with success • Uses a variety of sentence forms for effect • Mostly uses Standard English appropriately with mostly controlled grammatical structures • Generally accurate spelling, including complex and irregular words • Increasingly sophisticated use of vocabulary
Level 2 5–8 marks	• Sentence demarcation is mostly secure and sometimes accurate • Some control of a range of punctuation • Attempts a variety of sentence forms • Some use of Standard English with some control of agreement • Some accurate spelling of more complex words • Varied use of vocabulary
Level 1 1–4 marks	• Occasional use of sentence demarcation • Some evidence of conscious punctuation • Simple range of sentence forms • Occasional use of Standard English with limited control of agreement • Accurate basic spelling • Simple use of vocabulary

Sample Response:

In my opinion, the Royal family should definitely be abolished. There are far too many of them: earls and duchesses and princes and princesses. From what I can see, they do very little apart from going round the country in luxury cars, shaking hands with people, opening the occasional bridge, meeting charity workers and telling them they are doing a good job for free and having gourmet meals. Wouldn't we all like a job like that? Seriously – what would we miss if they were not there? We have plenty of politicians who already do things like that so therefore we don't need the Royal family. And it would be far cheaper for the taxpayer without having to keep them all in their palaces, pay for their expensive wardrobes and their transport.

I know people say that they are part of our tradition but why should we keep a tradition that is so old fashioned and out of date? We no longer put people in the stocks, have workhouses, cut people's hands off for stealing. These were all traditions too but we have got rid of them because they just were not fair. So, it is also not fair that just because you were born into a particular family, you should have so much when lots of other people today really struggle to make a living.

In addition, all that money that is spent on soldiers and police guarding them could be spent on other things in our communities. People are always complaining there are not enough police when there is crime in your local area, or that hospitals need more money and staff. We all know that the country is in debt and politicians keep telling us that cuts have to be made to important things such as the NHS and yet we still have enough money to have guards in fancy uniforms and security staff for the royals.

If we didn't have to pay for the Royal family and their luxury palaces, we could use the money spent on them for the NHS, education and to get homeless people off the street and into proper housing. Why should they have so many huge houses and palaces? You can only live in one place at any one time. I think we should get rid of the Royal Family and their palaces and big houses and use the funds for local communities so that everybody has a fairer chance in life.

States a clear point of view and uses some listing for effect.

Shows an awareness of the audience for the speech with the use of the rhetorical questions.

Uses a counter argument to introduce a new idea.

Makes an interesting comparison to develop the argument.

Uses discourse marker to develop the argument further.

Varies the structure of the sentences for interest and effect.

Makes a clear concluding sentence.

Commentary

There is a clear attempt made here to meet the purpose of arguing in a debate. There is a range of ideas offered in appropriate paragraphs. There is some use of structural features – a simple introductory statement and conclusion as well as the introduction of a counter argument.

The register or tone feels just about right for a speech delivered to college students. The vocabulary is quite straightforward but there are some interesting touches such as the rhetorical questions and the use of humour in places, which adds some interest and a personal voice, which is still controlled.

The sentence punctuation is accurate and there is some control of a range of punctuation, such as question marks, commas and dashes. Sentences are varied in the way they are constructed and Standard English is used throughout.

My checklist for success

When I answer this question I need to remember to:

- _____
- _____
- _____
- _____

Notes

Notes